CONFESSIONS
of a
CHURCH FINANCIAL SECRETARY

The Truth About Tithing:
An Eyewitness Account
(And...What Your Preacher Won't Tell You!)

LYN JOHNSTON TAKEN

XULON PRESS

Xulon Press
2301 Lucien Way #415
Maitland, FL 32751
407.339.4217
www.xulonpress.com

Printed in the United States of America.

Paperback ISBN-13: 978-1-66281-441-9
Ebook ISBN-13: 978-1-66281-442-6

TABLE OF CONTENTS

INTRODUCTION

YOU HAVE JUST PICKED UP A BOOK WRITTEN BY a skeptic.

I am a believer in the Bible, but there are areas where I still have questions and doubts—things I don't understand. Like everyone, we all wonder about things like pain and suffering, good and evil, faith and hypocrisy; why some people seem to get healing while others do not; unanswered prayers; even death itself.

One characteristic my family helped instill in me is a sense of curiosity. They taught me to look under the surface and not just believe something because it's what I've been told, or because it's what the crowd believes. I was taught to search and dig for truth. Therefore, I consider myself a "skeptical believer."

As long as I can remember, I've had this skeptical streak in me. I don't always take things at face value. I think this trait developed in me due to the openness and curiosity with which my family has always approached the Bible and life itself. It is where I learned that perhaps our own beliefs could possibly be wrong. We must check our own views, examine *why* we have come to these conclusions, and review them constantly.

Sometimes our views can be changed when we listen to the experiences of others. For example, I was skeptical about Acts 8:38-40. This is where Phillip baptized the Ethiopian eunuch, and, after he baptized him, "the Spirit of the Lord carried Phillip away, and the eunuch saw him no more... But Phillip found himself at Azotus." What? "The Sprit carried him away"? Am I reading that right?

Some years ago, I told a friend of mine that I could not believe that Phillip was just "magically transported" to another place.

I am so glad I told her of this particular doubt because she shared with me a personal story of something similar to Phillip's "journey" that had happened to her.

Had I not been friends with her, respected her, and known she had no reason to make up such a story, I would probably still be in unbelief about Phillip's "Star-Trek-like" transport.

But I *did* have reason to believe her. I believe her experience was real, not a dream nor something she made up.

I had even pointed out that for whatever reason, I could believe that Jesus died and rose from the dead, but I couldn't believe "this Phillip story."

Now I do, because of her; her experience, and her sharing it with me, it strengthened my faith.

One of the general themes taught in the Bible (though sometimes, there are miraculous exceptions, such as the one just mentioned) is that there are certain laws in life that are "sure things." For example, we believe in the law of gravity. We have experienced it, and we've learned about it in school.

There are laws in biology, chemistry, mathematics, nature, and science, the kinds of things we learned about while getting our education as children and young adults.

In nature, there are laws of sowing and reaping—that what we sow, we will grow. If you plant an apple seed, you will grow an apple tree—not an orange tree, not a fig tree. You will grow what you sow.

This book contains *my* story of what I saw as a church financial secretary—the differences I observed in the lives of consistent tithers versus the lives of those who only gave occasionally; how these observations impacted **me**; and how that impact changed my giving habits, my attitude, and my life.

It is my hope that my story will help strengthen your faith.

CHAPTER ONE

I MADE THE PIGGY BANK... BUT I MISSED THE POINT!

AS I BEGAN TO WRITE DOWN MEMORIES OF how tithing changed my life, I decided maybe I should share them. Experiences that others have shared with me have often changed my perspective and strengthened my faith. Only I can tell you what I saw with my own eyes and what I experienced concerning giving a tenth of my income to my local church. This discipline was greatly influenced by what I saw when I worked as a church financial secretary. But let me take you back a little further.

I was raised in church, and I remember making three little, paper-covered milk cartons labeled "church," "bank," and "house" in one of my Sunday school classes. These were our small "piggy banks," for helping us remember to put ten percent into the church one, ten percent into the bank (savings) one, and the remaining into the house one. We were taught to do this when we got our allowance/ chore money/ birthday money, etc.—"Give ten percent to the church and ten percent for your future, and the rest, you can spend on your needs and wants!" I'm sure the teachers went further into explaining the pros of tithing than I remember, but I mostly just wanted to make the prettiest stained-glass windows on my church bank. I wasn't very interested in why we were "supposed" to do these things with our money.

I don't remember hearing any preaching from the pulpit about tithing while I was growing up. Throughout my childhood, my teen years, and even through college, I don't recall any teaching on this particular subject. I even took notes in church, and I have never found any on the topic of tithing. I first began to hear about tithing when I started going to Harvest Cathedral in Macon, Georgia, in my thirties!

Back in 2002, when I joined Harvest Cathedral, there were seven classes that newcomers were encouraged to take. I remember the classes being similar to some of the things I had learned as a child and young adult in a Baptist setting, but there were also subjects that I would describe as being on a deeper level spiritually than many of the teachings I had learned while growing up. I felt the lessons went further into detail, things I had noticed in my own Bible study time, but had never heard mentioned in any of my Sunday school classes (or even in sermons). It was exciting to look forward to these lessons each Sunday. The ones I remember the most were "What We Believe" and "Tithing." Wow! My baby-kitten eyes were beginning to open—kinda late in life, but they were beginning to open!

Our pastor, Steve Sawyer, talked openly about tithing and how it had blessed his (and his family's) life, encouraging us to do so as well. I remember in one of his sermons, he talked about how giving consistently might be more important (initially) than being specific about giving a tenth (a tithe). He did emphasize the importance of a tenth, however, and that we should strive for giving at least that amount as we grew in this area of discipline.

He said that the main thing is to *start* giving—not your time, not your talents, but your money. You might not be at a point where you can give ten percent of your income, but maybe you can start with a ninth or a fifth or even, as he said, a "oneth." This was great motivation for me and gave me a starting point! The main thing is to start and be consistent. If you can only give one percent, or a "oneth," then *do it*. Start there if you have to and work up to a tenth.

CHAPTER TWO

I FELL IN LOVE
(WITH A CHURCH!)

WHEN I MOVED TO MACON, GEORGIA, IN EARLY 2002, I found the church that changed the way I looked at going to church. For many years it had become a lonely drudgery; I often left a service feeling lonelier than when I entered. I don't put the blame on the churches that I visited, as most of those years were very hard for me socially and emotionally. I had not attained the adulthood that I had dreamed of as a child, and even if I had found a church where I had felt that I fit in, I would have (more than likely) driven any potential close relationships/friendships away with my demeanor.

However, when I settled in Macon, in my search for a church home, I asked my neighbor Pat if he was a member of a congregation. His reaction is what sold me. Instead of just saying "Yes, I go to such-and-such church," he stopped, raised his eyebrows, and said with a big smile, "Yes! I do! I go to a church called "Harvest Cathedral" and I love it!" He seemed genuinely thrilled!

I found out where it was and visited, and I fell in love with Harvest Cathedral too! I had been a part of several different churches over the years, but this was different. I immediately felt I fit in, like it was home. There was a freedom and life that I felt pulsing from this extraordinary place and these friendly and open-hearted people that I had not found in any other church for many years. It was such an enjoyable church experience that I had a hard time waiting for Sunday mornings! I went to services every chance I could and even on Wednesday nights after being exhausted from work. Every service was like a celebration of God and of what Jesus had done for us. It was like a big production! I absolutely *loved* it. There were dancers, there were flags waving, banners lifted high (with extravagant workmanship and beauty) uplifting the various names of God, along with a diverse mix of musical styles a diverse congregation (racial, socioeconomic, and age) , and sound teaching communicated in a relaxed style. What drew me most was a sense of striving to accept one another no matter what point of your journey you were on. You were accepted and loved from the moment you walked in the door, *and* even as they got to know you! I noticed <u>everyone</u> of <u>every walk</u> was accepted and loved, right where they were.

It was during my first couple of months of attendance that the church, having become quite large, decided to start having home group meetings during the week. This is a shift that I have noticed is being talked about a lot lately due to the unique problems with what have become known as "mega churches."

This was also a huge blessing to me as a newcomer to the area. I was invited to visit different members' homes during the week, go out and eat, and just drop by. I have great memories of spending time with my church family, sometimes just playing cards together or going to a movie. I even remember one time when we were all doing karaoke to the Commodore's song "Brick House"!

We were all dancing the Electric Slide and singing and laughing. It was so much fun!

It was enriching to have contact with so many people during the week. Then, when we would get together at the physical church building, we were automatically drawn together. We weren't simply sitting in a row with people we didn't know. It made church, for the first time probably since my childhood, something I looked forward to each week.

During these years, I remember hearing Pastor Steve Sawyer talk about how "You can't out-give God," and how tithing had changed his and his family's life so much that he became almost obsessed with making sure he tithed on every single thing they were blessed to receive! I remember sort of thinking, *Well, I tithe, but I can't say it has changed my life.* That was my thought process. I did not question my own thought process about this at the time, thinking that my giving here and there was truly tithing. I would give a tenth for a period of time, not feel it was "working for me," and cut back or quit for a while.

CHAPTER THREE

NEW JOB... NEW MINDSET!

WHILE I WAS A MEMBER AT HARVEST CATHEDRAL, I began a new job at another church in the area, a large, quickly growing Baptist church. I was hired as the assistant to the financial director, and part of my job was to enter the contribution information into the computer system each week.

Working at the large Baptist church, day after day, week after week, I became steeped in budgets, contributions, purchases, bills, and donations—so much so that money was only numbers to me at work.

However, I started noticing something. After weeks and weeks and months and months, I started to realize that about twenty to thirty percent of the (active) members seemed to be truly consistent givers. Some, I could tell, made quite a bit of money; others not quite so much. Most, I could tell, just made modest incomes. But I could sort of judge from the amounts that these were true tithers. I could see that these people were serious about consistent tithing, and I began to notice something that really caught my attention.

I started noticing that the lives of these consistent tithers were different from the "here and there" givers. I had become acquainted with many of the members, even though this was not the church I was attending. Many would drop by to get literature for Sunday school; others I got to know because the women's ministry was quite active, and I was always invited to and included in their fellowships. These ladies made the fellowships inviting and comfortable. They loved to make things look and feel cozy. I enjoyed Christmastime when they would decorate tables in the fellowship hall for lunches and suppers. I knew some of these people better than I knew those with whom I attended church, simply from spending time with them during the week while I was at work.

I noticed (from my spy work) that the people who tithed on a regular basis did not seem to have the same chaos, constant life irritants, or devastation that the occasional givers had. I began noticing that tithers were more pleasant to be around and spend time with! This was a big eye-opener for me. I wanted to be this kind of person...someone... enjoyable! It was also becoming apparent to me, that it didn't matter the amount they gave; even if they didn't have much, the fact that they were consistent altered their lifestyle in a positive way.

Let me give you an example off the top of my head. I had heard of this "Grumpy Gus" who went to the church where I worked from several sources and had been informed, "If you ever encounter him, just brace yourself!" After my third warning about him, I decided to do some of my spy work! I looked up how long he had attended this church and saw that he had joined many years earlier. Since I had access, I decided to look up his tithing record. The folks who spoke of him seemed to think he was pretty well-set as a retiree, so I figured maybe tithing would be his redeeming quality. It was not. He had given *one* time a few years before and one time early on.

In contrast, I remember seeing a visitor at Harvest Cathedral who most of us single ladies were taking notice of! He was single, about my age, very considerate, and quite handsome! I admit, I wondered where he had come from since I had been at Harvest for several years at this point, I was involved in a "singles" life group, and I had never seen or heard of him, nor had anyone else! Eventually I understood that his wife had passed away, that he was searching for a new church home, and I put two and two together and remembered that our church had been praying for his wife (even though they were active in another church, but I didn't know which one).

A few months later I met him at a low country boil for some of the volunteers. He introduced himself to me as a newcomer to Harvest. He had a rare first name—I've only known one other person with this unique first name—and then he told me his last name and began spelling it out. However, there was no need for this because as soon as he said his last name, I pictured he and his wife's checks (from my years on the job at the Baptist church). I knew them well—brown checks with a black border with their name and address in calligraphy. I didn't interrupt him and let him spell out his last name for me, even though I wanted to say,

"Oh yes, I know you! You and your wife were consistent tithers at the church where I have worked for several years!" But of course, this was confidential information and I didn't feel it would be appropriate to blurt it out!

He had begun visiting Harvest Cathedral after his wife's passing, and he soon became planted there.

The difference in these two men was astounding. The Grumpy Gus who did not tithe consistently came into the office one day for change for a one-hundred-dollar bill. The receptionist called me on my intercom and asked if I could get him some change. I went out, he handed me the bill, and I turned to step into my office to get him change out of petty cash. He startled me by yelling out, "You don't walk off with _my_ money—you give it back to me, and you bring me change!" Stunned, I turned and handed him the bill, walked into my office, and retrieved the change within thirty seconds. I think he was a little embarrassed, not having realized that my office was right there and I would make the change so quickly. I numbly handed it to him, and he rudely recounted it out loud in front of me and the receptionist. Then, waving the bill as though it were a flag, handed me the hundred.

I was still shocked and stunned at his behavior. He didn't say thank you or anything else; he simply turned and walked out, almost as though he was proud of his behavior, that perhaps he had taught us some sort of lesson.

On the flip side of this, the consistent tither who had only recently lost his wife was such a nice fellow. Everyone at Harvest Cathedral took him in and enjoyed his company. He showed a deep faith in God in his demeanor and was generally just a pleasant guy to be around! He seemed genuinely interested in anyone who wanted to talk. He seemed to be a good listener, someone that anyone could relate to.

We at Harvest Cathedral would also have welcomed Grumpy Gus to our family, but thankfully (in my case), I am glad I had no more reasons to come face-to-face with old Grumpy!

I found this to be probably the widest scale of a tither versus a non-tither at the church where I worked (since I could truly observe and know who the tithers were and who were not tithers – and who the occasional givers were– and of course, the tippers!)—Grumpy Gus being at the lower end of the scale in many ways, and the recent widow at the other end of the scale. Even though he was going through something I cannot even imagine, he handled it with grace and courtesy to all of those around him.

Obviously, I don't know Grumpy Gus's story, and with his gruff nature, I didn't want to hear it! However, I point out these two ends of the spectrum as an example of the possible extremes of tithing versus non-tithing lifestyles (and mindsets) and what I observed on the job.

As a general observation of consistent tithers, I didn't see the friction that I saw in the non-consistent households, nor was there a "woe is me" cloud over the tithers' families in general. Not to say that the consistent tithers didn't have problems, because they did, but it didn't seem to rob them of their peace, nor did it seem to negatively effect their faith and trust in God as their supplier and protector. They seemed to be able to rest in times when I know that I would not have been able to remain so calm and assured! I was intrigued and began to wonder if this would work for me.

CHAPTER FOUR

OUCH! GUILTY! I WAS SHACKIN'... (AT CHURCH)

WHEN A COUPLE DECIDES TO LIVE TOGETHER without being married, y'all know we call that "shackin' up." In other words, either party is free to leave at any time for any reason. Generally, one person is more invested in the hope of the relation-ship working out (i.e. getting married). Of course, this is not always the case; I am only speaking in generalities.

One particular Sunday, Pastor Steve was talking about how if we wanted to go to a great confer-ence, or a concert, we would come up with the money to go. We understand that when it comes to something like this, there are costs involved. There is the expense of using the facility, the cost of cleaning, the bill for heating and cooling, the speaker's fee, the cost of the general maintenance needed to keep the building up and running (insurance, mortgage payments, etc.). However, we don't seem to think about this when we come into a nice, well-kept church building that was clean, air-conditioned, and heated, and where we got spiritually fed, got to meet new people, and got to talk and fellowship with our friends.

He pointed out, "Some of y'all are just 'shackin'. Y'all ain't helpin' pay the bills, y'all ain't pulling your weight—you're just shackin' here at the church, but you wouldn't do this anywhere else." Good point! We somehow figure out how to come up with money for the things we want to do. And I knew from paying the bills at my job that without consistent tithers, the church could not have stayed heated and cooled; we couldn't have kept the restroom facilities open; there would have been no cleaning crew or garbage pickup, and even little things would have been missing, like the coffee we enjoyed or the monthly calendar with planned activities. Then, of course, no preacher, no youth worker, no nursery, no preschool—you get the picture.

It was during this sermon that I realized I was not truly committed. I had been attending Harvest Cathedral at this time for about four years, and I gave occasionally. I did not like what I saw in my own attitude, so I wanted to make a change. I was going to take action and start tithing! I decided to be tenacious about it. I was no longer going to "shack up" and would "put God to the test," as the Bible says in Malachi 3:10. I was finally going to give consistently and not just here and there.

CHAPTER FIVE

THE CHARISMATIC EXPERIENCE

EVEN THOUGH MOST OF MY LIFE GROWING UP (and in college) I had joined and attended Baptist churches, I had always visited and appreciated other church denominations as well.

When I was younger, my parents would let me visit church with my friend Dawn, whose family attended an Assemblies of God church.

From my first visit, I really loved this church. I loved the congregants' open expression of their love for God. I enjoyed their worship style, the music, and the freedom of raising their hands and even some jumping around!

Having been raised in a family that believed in "balance" in life, I realized there was a balance between these two church atmospheres, and I liked and appreciated both.

I noticed there were some at the Assemblies of God church who were standing still, some who were moving around and swaying or raising their hands, and some who were sitting. I didn't see any obvious judgement toward or between any of the groups. I really enjoyed this church family, and I especially enjoyed Vacation Bible School (we did lots of arts and crafts).

I bring up this early experience to say that I believe it is a beautiful thing when we can be expressive in our love for God. However, everyone is not made this way. Not everyone is an expressive person.

If you have read any books on personality, you know there are four basic personality types. (Some books go into more detail, but generally they start with four basic types.) Most people are not just one type all together; most of us are a mixture of at least two. We generally have a mixture of all the types, but have more natural tendencies in one or two areas.

I enjoy moving around a little, especially when I hear music with a good beat! However, I knew

that this was not really encouraged in a Baptist setting. But at Dawn's church, I could move around
and enjoy this newfound "freedom" of worship.

Interestingly, I've noticed, as I've been around
charismatic churches more often over the years,
that there sometimes tends to be a bit of under-
lying attitude that someone might not be as "spiritual" as another person if he or she isn't expressive
during the worship portion of the service. This was
something I didn't notice as a child when visiting
the Assemblies of God church with my friend.

I know a lot of people who I would turn to if I
was in great need, some of whom do not attend
a charismatic church. They don't raise their hands
during the song portion, and they might not even
say "Amen" out loud when most of the rest of the
congregation does.

There are strong and solid people who I know
and love, rocks who will be there for me if I need
them. They may not dance around to the music or
"look" spiritual to others, but I have been around
them long enough to know they are the real deal.
They believe, and they live out their belief in the
Bible and in the Lord. They are also more than likely

consistent tithers in many churches—at least this was the case in the church where I worked.

There were, of course, even some at the Baptist church that I knew were more on the "Bapticostal" side, and were more inclined to say amen, to raise their hands, etc., and many of them were also consistent tithers. I hope it is clear that I am not trying to say that just because someone is charismatic means they don't tithe! I just happened to notice, over many years, that often the ones that are "overlooked"—perhaps due to their personality not fitting into some sort of mold that we humans have made up in our own minds—were often the steady, unwavering tithers of the church where I worked.

Without them, your church might not be able to keep the doors open. It saddens me to see a small, rural church be forced to close. Even though the building has been paid off for many years, the congregation may have been raised, like me, without a lot of teaching on tithing.

If that small congregation only has ten active members, that means probably one or two families are carrying the church. If they leave, the church will soon close its doors.

If everyone would consistently tithe (give ten percent of their income), this would not happen; these small, rural churches would not end up putting "For Sale" signs in their front yards.

In Malachi, it's pretty straightforward that this is an area where we are encouraged to "test" God! (This test is for our sake, not for God's.) It is to prove to us that He will keep His word. It is not a magic formula, and we have to bear in mind that Malachi was talking to farmers. They understood the seasons in farming. They knew there were times of planting, times of waiting, times of rain, times of drought, but there were also times of harvest. But they knew if they planted a seed today, it would take time for it to grow, it would have to be tended to, and it would have to be harvested at the right time.

The book of Malachi is different than any other book. In it, God had a back-and-forth conversation with His people. He told them how they were taking care of their own homes but not His house.

He talked about the curse they were under as a result of not giving to Him, and how they were robbing Him; How their whole nation was under a curse because of their lack of concern for His house.

Of course, they acted innocent and asked, "How are we robbing you?" and He told them that they were robbing Him in tithes and offerings. He also told them that this was the reason they were living under a curse.

Have you ever felt like you were living under a curse? I certainly have. Until I began tithing consistently—until I gave it some time (seasons)—I could never get ahead, no matter how hard I worked! My attitude was "woe is me," and even though I didn't want to be that way, that attitude reigned in my life. I really wanted to change, and I noticed that this attitude did not reign in the consistent tithers' lives! My reasons for tithing consistently were beginning to add up! The consistent tithers had what I wanted, and I was beginning to understand that I was the one that had to set this in motion. No one else could do it for me. Prayer wasn't going to do it, fasting wouldn't write out a check for me, a better job wasn't going to permanently fix the heart of the problem, and trying to change my own attitudes wasn't going to do it! I had to be the one to start tithing, and keep tithing.

CHAPTER SIX

EXPOSING WHAT YOUR PREACHER WON'T TELL YOU.

"MAKE YOUR BEST DOUBLE CHIN FOR ME, LYN." This is what Donna, my physical therapist, told me during my second session. I made my best double chin, and I could immediately tell why I needed to do it. I was in physical therapy for my shoulder, and I felt something in that whole general area, a letting-go of sorts, as I did this stretch.

There was a law of muscles and muscle groups involved. Since I have had no training in this area, I had no idea this would help me. I didn't have the knowledge that if I did this double-chin stretch, it would help free up my shoulder. But Donna knew because she had studied these laws of muscle groups, and she has helped many patients with their injuries—if they will follow her directions!

I was impressed! Something so simple yet with great results. Of course, there were many other stretches and exercises we did for my shoulder, but would I have ever thought to make a double chin to help ease my pain? This was amazing to me!

When something has helped me, *especially* when something has changed my **life**, I want to tell the world about it. If you have a problem and I know of a solution, something that helped me, I want to tell you about it so that it can help you too!

But, that doesn't mean you want to hear what I have to say!

I have given advice that has been totally ignored, and I bet you have, too.

As it is with your pastor.

There are things that your pastor probably will not tell you because he has given advice many times only to be ignored; perhaps some have even been offended at his teaching, particularly on tithing (believing he was merely looking out for his own salary).

Tithing is one of those areas that I find diffi-cult to talk about with others (and I'm not even a preacher)! If I know the person I am talking to also has experience of the deep truth of tithing, then it can be a deep and enjoyable conversation. I can freely talk about tithing to those who I know already understand the changes it produces in your life and, more importantly, in your attitudes. But trying to talk to someone who has not embraced this concept is uncomfortable and often feels like a wasted attempt to defend your position and what you know to be true.

However, tithing *is* biblical, so not only is the person hurting his or her own fiscal life by not tithing, he or she is also in rebellion against God—whether they realize it or not! This is part of the curse that you put **yourself** under by not tithing, no matter what your reasons may be.

Perhaps this is why I heard so few sermons on tithing. Your pastor *knows* that it can change your life. He has **seen** it change mindsets, but he knows you are hearing all the noise— the stories of the little old ladies who gave money to some televangelist. Yes, we have all heard them, and that is very unfortunate.

I mainly concentrate in this book on the subject of giving your tithe to your local church. I am not against giving to other ministries, but I believe that giving to your local church *first* (hopefully the one you attend regularly) is the system God has in place for not only blessing the tither and the particular church, but the city, and even the nation! Your local church should be the recipient of the first ten percent of your income—consistently.

Your pastor has the "cure for your financial cancer," but you find it hard to take from him. He's up there lookin' all dressy and comfortable, and he lives in that really nice community. He drives a nice car, his wife is dressed to the nines as are his kids, and maybe his kids are trouble with a capital "T"! But that doesn't mean he hasn't been through the mill to get to where he is.

All you are seeing is the product of his life, where he is right now. You have not seen the struggles, the sacrifices, the prayers, the on-bended-knee times, the pain, the grief, the dark places, and the heartache that have brought him to where he is today.

So, if your pastor dares preach on tithing, listen to him, and then follow through!

I found our pastor's words on tithing to be encouraging, not manipulative. I'm sure it can be a fine line for a preacher to try and teach on such a sensitive topic.

CHAPTER SEVEN

THIS WAS NOT THE LIFE I HAD DREAMED OF!

I RECENTLY BEGAN TO REALIZE THAT SO OFTEN when we pray for a blessing, what we really need is an inner change. We pray for things *around* us to change, but God wants to change us *inside* so that we can be stronger, more patient, and more understanding, so we have time and a reason to grow in faith. I believe that for most of us, this is the only way we will grow in spiritual maturity. During much of my life, when I was struggling (financially in particular), I prayed for a "blessing." God, however, had much better plans for me, though it did not *feel* like it at the time! Occasionally, He does drop that sweet blessing into our laps, but more often than not He would rather change our hearts, minds, attitudes, and appetites than change our circumstances. When He does this, it changes our *entire* lives, not just the temporary situations we might find ourselves facing at the moment. Sort of like the old saying: "Give a man a fish and he will eat for a day. Teach a man to fish, and he will eat for a lifetime." God is trying to teach us, and strengthen us, by not always rescuing us from our immediate and pressing circumstances. He wants to teach us how to live. He wants us to learn that we can trust Him. It has been a hard (and constantly ongoing) lesson for me, a hard-headed skeptic!

I was so blessed to have been born into the family I was—a gentle, loving, disciplined, God-fearing, God-loving family with a fantastic sense of humor! My brother, parents, grandparents, aunts, uncles, cousins, neighbors, schoolteachers, and church leaders were the best I could have asked for! I admit, I hit the lottery when it came to my upbringing!

However, even with the best upbringing and the best examples, we do not always fall into the place we had hoped and prayed for in our earlier lives.

Sometimes we find ourselves very disappointed with our lives, saying, "Hey, God, this isn't the life I dreamed of!" Things were not turning out the way I wanted. As a child, I wanted to get married at a young age—I'm talking first grade!

I had fallen in love with the cutest, blonde-haired boy I had ever seen. I can remember asking my mother if I could marry him, and she told me I could marry anyone I wanted to. I don't think she realized I wanted a wedding in June of *that* year, but in my young and innocent brain, I did, and it seemed perfectly logical to me. I knew couples in our church who had been married fifty years, so in my six-year-old, mathematically-challenged mind, I thought they must have gotten married in first or second grade.

Needless to say, I had a strong desire to get married from an incredibly young age. After high school, though, I wanted to live the life of Mary Richards from *The Mary Tyler Moore Show* or Ann Marie on *That Girl*. I wanted to be the independent, good-looking girl who could make it on her own and then, around twenty-seven, get married and have a *Brady Bunch* life!

Ironically, I didn't marry until I was forty-eight years old. I was never able to "make it on my own" (like Mary and Ann), at least not very well, and constantly struggled financially, emotionally, and socially. (Definitely not the life I had dreamed!) I had not hoped to be single all those years. It was not the life I ever thought I would have.

CHAPTER EIGHT

NO...I DID NOT TITHE.

THE YEARS BETWEEN HIGH SCHOOL AND COL-
lege, and the years after college as well, were
very awkward and difficult. I longed for a mate
who I could not find, while also trying to navigate
becoming an adult.

I endured so many bad jobs—jobs I hated.
I worked at one place where every Monday
morning as I drove up I would hope the building
had burned down during the night. You might say
I despised that job! Not only that, but the pay was
so bad that it barely covered my rent each month.
I was too determined to be "out on my own" to
get a roommate, a decision that if I could do over,
I would opt for a roomie. I made my own way

difficult, but somehow, I stumbled through those most difficult years.

Having been raised in church, I always sought out a church home wherever I lived. I desired to be with like-minded believers, but I always felt like I didn't fit in. Most of those my age were married, and some were married with babies. I was too old for the college crowd and too young for the divorced crowd!

I can remember how much I struggled financially during that time. I made a comment about it once to a small church group, and they tried to think of better places I could work, especially so I wouldn't have to keep putting my groceries, doctor's bills, and gas on a credit card!

Someone would mention a place that might be hiring; others told me about where they worked and if they had an opening for this or that. It was during these suggestions I remember one lady asking, "Do you tithe?" The discussion kept going amongst those who were brainstorming better places of employment, and I remember wanting to ask her why she had asked me that. No, I did not—not really. I was probably "tipping" but was not consistently giving ten percent of my income to my local church. I think she knew the "secret" of tithing! <u>Even though I was in regular church attendance, I still was not hearing any teaching on tithing.</u> I wish I would have halted the conversation and asked her *why* she had asked me that particular question.

Sadly, I was not the only person who was not being taught about tithing. It appears to me that an entire generation is trying to ride the coat tails of earlier age groups that understood the value of the discipline of consistent tithing.

As a child and teenager, I saw our city flourish. I saw neighborhoods bounding with energy. Our schools were full, almost overflowing with students; the local churches were incredibly active, thriving, with all age groups involved in various activities.

I saw our town as it buzzed along with two cotton mills, many sewing factories, a blue jeans stone-washing facility, restaurants, downtown businesses, a movie theater, full of working class people with steady jobs that paid a living wage. Of course, it was not without problems, but I point these things out to show the differences from then to now—how not only has the economy changed, but how the attitudes and mindsets of the generations are changing. We have moved away from church life, and especially from taking care of the church through consistent tithing.

Grievously, the cotton mills, along with the sewing factories, are all closed, with the exception of one small factory still in operation. My hometown has changed, but not just my small hometown... other places I have lived have suffered many industrial losses over the last thirty years that have affected all of the other industry in the areas.

Thankfully, the people of Opp, Alabama (my hometown) have smart, innovative leadership, council people, local businesses, and others, that are trying to think of new ways to bring industry to the area. But it is difficult.

Where there used to be hundreds of people working directly for one of the two cotton mills, or even thousands employed indirectly (sewing factories, restaurants, clothing stores, shoe stores, real estate, doctor's offices, etc.), the population has dwindled to almost half of when I left in the 1980s.

I realize the seemingly obvious reasons for the downturn. Things changed drastically in the 1980s regarding trade in America, Mexico, and China.

I remember loving the "cheap" stuff we could finally get! What bargains! But at what price?

I'm going to make a profound statement (in the form of a question). As Zig Ziglar would say... I'm telling you ahead of time that it's a profound statement, so you'll *know* it's a profound statement!

I can't help but wonder, if my generation had been tithing—if we had understood the promises, the principles, the benefits of consistent tithing, if we had taken care of God's house—would we have made wiser decisions as a nation?

Of course, I do not know the answer to my own profound question. However, I do know that we need to take the care of God's house seriously, and we have not done this.

I desire for my hometown to be fiscally and spiritually bountiful! I desire my city, county, state, and my nation to thrive! God, through Malachi, tells us how to become a nation that is blessed! I believe it is time that we listen and take action.

CHAPTER NINE

WHY SHOULD WE LET YOU IN?

WHEN I WAS GROWING UP, THE CHURCH I attended with my family was what I consider a dedicated learning church. Sunday School, Training Union, Vacation Bible School, Royal Ambassadors, and mission-minded Girls in Action were a mainstay for gaining knowledge about the Bible, God, missionaries, and even about ourselves. There were also lots of family fellowships, catching and frying fish at a local lake, covered dish suppers, adventures for kids and teens, and all of this was led by creative, sweet, faithful, trustworthy, and fun Christian examples.

We learned that God is perfect and that all generations had to have a sacrifice to be able to approach God.

In the Old Testament, they used birds and goats and other animals, as sacrifices. I heard a preacher once talk about how he had wondered why these animals were "good enough" to be a sacrifice to God. I had wondered too, so I really took note of his answer.

He conjectured (and I agree) that animals are the only things that God created that actually "do" what He created them to do! They do not rebel against it. A tiger chases down a gazelle because that's what God made him to do. Birds sing and chirp, build their nests, and teach their young to fly. They don't get up one morning and think, "I'm not going to chirp today. I know I was made to chirp, but I'm not going to, not today."

In this sense, animals are pure and innocent. They do not rebel against their maker. Therefore, they were able to be presented as a sacrifice for man's sins under the old covenant.

But praise the Lord—He provided Jesus, His perfect Son, as our sacrifice under the new covenant. I'm so relieved that I don't have to kill birds or goats or any other animals, on a weekly, monthly, or yearly basis, to atone for my sins!

I remember what I consider one of Pastor Steve's best illustrations. He brought up the old proverbial question: "If you were to die tonight and were at the gates of heaven, and Saint Peter asked, 'Why should I let you in?' what would you say?"

Pastor Steve said, "Don't say, 'Because I was a member of Harvest Cathedral,' 'Because I got baptized,' 'Because I'm a good person, 'Because I walked the aisle at my church when I was twelve'— don't say, 'Because I anything.' The only answer is, 'Jesus.' If they ask why they should let you in, just say, 'Jesus.' If they ask you anything at the gate, just say, 'Jesus'!"

What a simple and deep truth, but we complicate it by turning it into salvation depending on our actions.

Even though I had heard the message of salvation my whole life, understood it, and believed it, I finally realized that when God looks at you (or me), He looks *through* what Jesus has done for you. This illustration simplified the gospel for me, and I couldn't hear it enough!

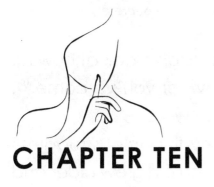

CHAPTER TEN

THE RISE OF TELEVANGELISM

I UNDERSTOOD MY NEED FOR A SAVIOR AND was convicted of my sinful nature at a revival service when I was twelve years old. I was eager to learn about all areas of life, but other than salvation, what other subjects could I learn about from the Bible, to have a spiritual perspective on them? What about the other areas of blessing and knowledge? What about how to live day-to-day? This is where we take our head knowledge of things we learned in Sunday school and from studying the Bible and put them into practice. I am certainly not perfect, and often feel like a hypocrite. I can totally believe what I know to be true about God, then turn right back around and be in momentary doubt! However, as I've heard said about faith, and about growing in faith, "Don't look at how far you have to go, look at how far you've come." I often remind myself of these words.

But what about all of my financial struggles? Why was I constantly struggling as I grew older and went out on my own? I was budgeting and sticking to that budget, but I was still short every month.

It was the law of sowing and reaping that I needed to understand. No, I could not have given much in those early years— my tithe would have been a small amount of money—but to me, at that time, I thought I needed to hang on to it. However, this was a law that I had to set in motion. I had to be the one to start and continue to tithe, but I was clueless.

I believe that because of the lack of teaching (on tithing) to perhaps an entire generation, the rise of televangelism set up my generation (and others who were untaught and uneducated in this area), to be primed for giving some of our earnings to strangers in a desperate attempt to put ourselves under the blessing that God promised His people in the book of Malachi.

Unfortunately, some gave all their savings to some of the illegitimate, early-on televangelists.

The airwaves were ripe with many who were mere charlatans, using this new route of making money.

I fell for this but, thankfully, only one time. While I should have been tithing to my own church, I was not. One very soft-spoken TV preacher (not as well-known as some but long off the air now) convinced me and millions of others to send in a one-time gift of $100. This was a huge amount for me, but in my desperation, I scraped it together. We were promised by this stranger that if we did this, we would receive a huge financial blessing from God, then to throw in just enough Scripture to bait me he recited from Malachi where God said He would "pour out such a blessing on you that you will not have room enough to contain it."

When I look back at this time period of my life, it's hard to believe that I still was not hearing any teaching on the subject of tithing! The televangelists were the only ones talking about money and about giving! I knew the Bible taught about giving, but I was still wandering in ignorance, and I was in regular church attendance!

This was in the late eighties and early nineties. I am thankful for and believe that most of the shady characters of televangelism have been weeded out and accountability has been enforced, but has the church dropped the ball on teaching about tithing?

CHAPTER ELEVEN

CHALLENGE ACCEPTED!

WE WILL LEAVE THE EIGHTIES AND NINETIES behind and talk about the 2000s, Harvest Cathedral, and working at the large Baptist church. I was observing the obvious differences in the lives of tithers versus non-tithers, and my mindset was changing. It was around this time that Sam Drye, the bishop of our church (whose dream and hard work birthed Harvest Cathedral), gave out a challenge.

One Sunday, he was talking about how there is something in us humans that wants to be religious in some area of our lives. He described what the word "religious" meant and how we can be religious towards anything, it doesn't have to be something associated with spirituality. He said some folks clean their cars, religiously (especially if they have a rare or vintage vehicle). Some folks cut their lawn, religiously. Most of us folks have certain things we do religiously (that everyone needs to do religiously), such as brushing our teeth, bathing, any and all routines that keep us smelling fresh! We all got a good laugh but were beginning to understand what he was saying.

He was talking about religion versus relationship. He said "I can sit down and read my Bible for eight hours a day, but that doesn't mean I have a stronger relationship with God than I had before I started on my religious reading session". He was pointing out that though time spent reading the Bible is very important, it is more important that we let it speak to our hearts, allow it to change us through the power of God, than just to spend the time reading...just to spend the time...for time's sake. We have to be attentive to the still, small, voice when it tries to speak to us. We have to pay attention, and we have to be responsive. This is where relationship comes into the picture.

God always desired to have relationship with mankind. However, mankind rebelled and even though God went looking for Adam in the garden

("Adam, where are you?") Adam (mankind) hid himself from God (or so he thought). Relationship was God's idea. Religion is man's idea. Religion is man's way of trying to be "good enough" to approach God. Look at all of the laws and rules and regulations that man came up with (after the rebellion of man against God) in the old testament! Look at the Levitical laws! There was no way anyone could live up to these exceedingly high expectations and rules! No way!

He spoke about how we try and substitute *religion* for *relationship*. He explained that in many ways religion is easier. We can check things off our list, pat ourselves on the back, and be "done" for the day. I've read my bible...check! I've prayed...check! I've helped at the soup kitchen...check!

We don't have to relate to anyone to have religion. Religion is all about what WE do. It's about keeping the car clean, keeping the lawn mowed, about keeping our breath fresh! As Christians it can become about attending church, about helping the less fortunate, about trying to "win souls". We can become quite prideful about religion. It's a different story with relationship. It involves listening, often listening when we don't want to listen, often moving our lives around for someone else, it involves humility, and vulnerability.

Bishop Sam said: "I don't believe in being religious—except when it comes to tithing" (laughter from the congregation ensued). He explained that one of the areas where being religious in church will literally and figuratively "pay off" is in tithing. He never guaranteed we'd get rich if we tithed religiously, but he explained how our lives would change. There is a trust involved in tithing consistently (religiously), and your trust will grow. Your life will become fuller and more satisfying because you are showing, no...you are proving to yourself, that you trust God!

Then he said, "If you *really* want to be religious about something, be religious about tithing!"

"I believe in tithing *so much* that if you will consistently tithe for one year, and you can come to me after a year and tell me that your life is not better after tithing consistently, I will make sure you get your money back."

With this endorsement and what I had begun to see on my job at the Baptist church, I decided to take his challenge, knowing fully well that I would not need to get my money back at the end of the year.

CHAPTER TWELVE

CHANGE DID NOT COME QUICKLY, BUT IT CAME

IT WOULD BE NICE TO SAY THAT AS SOON AS I began this journey, my life changed and became much easier immediately, especially financially! But that was not the case. I still went through some really tough times. I was paying off credit cards that I had used in those really lean times in my life. I had accumulated around $14,000 in credit card debt that I had been making payments on for years. It took me many years to pay off that balance!

But I did begin to notice that my life was becoming a bit easier a little at a time. My hairstylist began giving me free eggs, as well as any excess vegetables that she had grown and couldn't use. I was asked by a trusted friend if I wanted a "boarder" to rent a room in my home. This friend knew this gal who was trustworthy, so she moved in. We got along great! This was a blessing I had not dreamed of, and it took a big burden off my shoulders. Other blessings began to accumulate as it was also about this time that I finished paying off my car! This gave me an additional $213.14 a month to put toward my credit card debt.

I've heard debates on the subject of tithing and how it is no longer necessary to practice giving ten percent of your income to your local church since we are now "under the new covenant" and that "outdated, antiquated practice was under the old (law)."

But things had begun to turn around in my life since I committed to tithing consistently. Because of what I was seeing on my job at the Baptist church, I knew that tithing is something that we can do that sets certain things into motion in our lives. Just like when we sow mercy, we receive mercy, and when we sow understanding, we receive understanding. We might sow these things way before we enjoy their fruit. Just because we plant mercy to a specific individual does not mean we will receive mercy from that *particular person*. But at some other point in our life, we may not even realize that we have done something for which we deserve correction, disciplinary action, or a good receiving of a "piece of someone's mind"! Later, we usually look back and realize times when we have received undeserved mercy, grace, and forgiveness from others.

The discipline of tithing helps to break us free from habits and attitudes that are destructive. I began to realize this was happening in my life, and I wasn't "trying" to change my attitudes, it was just happening! We become more grateful, and we appreciate the small blessings more. We begin to see the work of our hands actually profiting and not all being eaten up by locusts... and see that the holes are no longer in our purse!

You will notice these things adding up, and you will notice your attitudes changing. My attitudes were finally becoming more like the tithers I admired from my "intel" on my job. I felt a softening in my spirit and a change in the way I looked at those who were in financially stable families. I realized the ones I was observing weren't necessarily all from "old money." It was their attitude towards keeping their church financially sound, and carefully stewarding what they had been entrusted with that made the difference. There was a humility about them.

I know we all wish our ship would come in; we wish we would find out we got left out of a family inheritance from years back, or we won the lottery or some other form of receiving a lot of money at one time. We tend to think if we could just get that "big boatload of money" we'd be fine! However... if you have ever watched any documentaries investigating the lives of multi-million-dollar lottery winners in the years after they win big bucks, you'll know that just having a lot of money does not bring peace! The documentaries that I have seen show that most multi-million-dollar lottery winners end up broke, in debt, filing for bankruptcy, or *dead*, usually within five years of their big win!

Therefore, I believe God *does* want to bless us, even with finances, but not *only* with money because that would not truly be a blessing; it would be a burden.

I have seen God's system at work, and I admired the people that trusted and respected that system. They were faithful in giving. They were standing in faith. They understood the laws of tithing.

CHAPTER THIRTEEN

NOT SCREAMING OR YELLING—JUST STANDING

I WAS INVITED TO A SUPPER AND PRAYER MEETING at a friend-of-a-friend's home. I didn't know this friend-of-a-friend and was convinced to go because of her compelling argument: "There will be food!"

So after enjoying a nice meal, we stood around the table, hands held, and our host asked if anyone would like to pray. There were a couple of sweet prayers, and then our host began praying—okay, she began yelling! She worked up to an all-out scream, telling the devil that he had to leave someone (I don't remember the specifics) alone!

This yelling and screaming went on and on, with most of the others giving words of agreement; "Yes,

Lord, keep the enemy's hands off of so-and-so." I stood there wishing I could slip out, but I could not as my hands were clasped by those on each side of me!

Was her screaming effective? I don't know. I never asked for an update on the individuals she was praying for.

Maybe it was! But I don't know that it's a biblically encouraged state of spiritual warfare.

Having done a good bit of study through the years, I feel I have noticed a couple of recurring themes, none of which involve yelling at demons, the devil, or any of our enemies.

Often the person is encouraged to not be afraid, but to be courageous, and often to "just stand."

I've never been a fan of standing up in one place for long (or even short) periods of time. It has always really made my legs and body hurt. However, it seems like most every job I had growing up (and then in college) required hours of standing—not a lot of walking around, just a lot of standing in one general area.

The Bible talks about "standing."

Ephesians 6:13 says, "Therefore, put on the full armor of God, so that when the day of evil comes, you may be able to stand your ground, and after you have done everything, to stand."

Yet, we hate to stand. Standing usually implies that we are waiting, and we are typically waiting in line—usually to pay for something! Whether it's getting the tag for our car or buying our groceries or cleaning supplies or clothes, there is usually some physical standing involved. Occasionally, we are standing in line to ride a roller coaster or some other form of entertainment, but whatever we are doing, when we are standing, it is not fun and is uncomfortable!

So it is with "standing" in our faith. We generally do not like it, and it is usually unpleasant and diffi-cult. We will do almost anything to get out of this area of discipline because we want the easy way out. We would rather cry and scream at the devil than *stand*. Our flesh, even the part required to "stand" spiritually, is lazy.

I want to suggest this to you—when you tithe, you are standing in faith against the evil forces in your life. I have seen this "standing" break down attitudes in my own life and have watched it change my income from all going to pay bills... to me having extra and being able to enjoy my life outside of work, as well as my work life! Most of all, I have seen the amazing and unexplainable difference it has made, though slowly, and steadily, in my life and attitudes.

We can sometimes be so moved by a song or a sermon that we might raise our hands in worship, but how about raising my pen and writing a check to my local church **during the week** when I might not be in a "worshipful" mood?

From what I have observed from consistent tithers and what I have seen in my own life, this tenacity not only made a difference in their lives financially—it went so much deeper. They were <u>standing</u>. They were benefiting from the domino effect of tithing consistently, *and* they didn't have to yell at the pests that had been destroying their crops; the Lord was rebuking the devourers *for* them!

I was ready to be one of them!

CHAPTER FOURTEEN

EITHER YOU BELIEVE IT...OR YOU DON'T!

AS MY DADDY SAYS (CONCERNING SCRIPTURE in particular), "Either you believe it, or you don't!" My daddy, with his God -given personality of setting his face like flint and doing whatever he says he will do, has always been a picture of great faith and discipline for me. When he believes, he is all-in. My mother remembers when daddy smoked cigarettes. She would buy them when she bought groceries. She said one day he told her not to buy him any more cigarettes. She asked him why, and he had read that it was believed that second-hand smoke was bad for babies (she was pregnant with my brother in 1961) and so he was going to quit. That was it. No tapering off, no counseling classes, no hypnosis, no nicotine patches (ok, not that they existed back then, but you get my point), no back-up plan. He quit cold turkey. I remember my uncles talking about how Daddy used to smoke not just any cigarettes—according to them, he smoked the "strong stuff" (and named off a particular brand). He decided to quit because he wanted to protect his soon-to-be-born son, and he *believed* what he had read about the dangers of cigarette smoke.

If we believe something, we believe it in its entirety! Then we act on it. If we don't believe something, we won't act on it, because there is not enough evidence, at least in our mind, to move us in that particular direction. We *might* dip our toe in, but we will not be consistently moving in a certain direction if we don't believe that it will have a rewarding outcome, or if we don't see results right away.

I *thought* I believed in tithing. I *thought* I was a true tither. When I began to give careful thought to my ways regarding this, I realized then that I was not a true tither. I also realized that I did not believe in the benefits of tithing! (Think back to my inner thoughts I shared earlier when Pastor Steve would say, "You can't out-give God.") I am so grateful to have been given the opportunity to see for myself the benefits in the lives of true, believing, consistent tithers.

I *thought* I believed in it, until I put myself to the test. Things got rough. I decided to push through! I was not going to do like I had in the past and stop for a period of time. Because of the teaching I was hearing, and what I was seeing with my own eyes, I kept at it. I kept giving. When I put myself to the test, when I decided to quit "shackin' up at church," when I decided to be consistent *no matter what...* that's when I had other breakthroughs in my life. I think that all of our reactions (and reasons) for not tithing stem from either a lack of knowledge, or a lack of faith.

Are you like I was? Do you start tithing, only to give up after a certain amount of time? Just like God promised to open the heavens and rebuke the devourer for the farmers He was talking to in Malachi, those farmers knew there were still **seasons**. They knew they still had to work—to do the tilling and the planting and the waiting.

I certainly hope my experience as a church financial secretary, and what I observed in that position, will help motivate you to begin, and continue, tithing. If you are already a consistent tither, I hope my words have helped encourage you for your faithful giving.

If you're still having a difficult time in starting your tithing journey, perhaps you can take my husband's advice and, as he likes to say, try a little faith!

> "And without faith, it is impossible to please God, because anyone who comes to Him must believe that He exists, and that he rewards those who earnestly seek Him." (Hebrews 11:6)

CHAPTER FIFTEEN

"YOURS WILL BE A DELIGHTFUL LAND."

Bring the whole tithe into the store-house, that there may be food in my house. **Test me in this," says the Lord Almighty, "and see if I will not throw open the floodgates of heaven and pour out so much blessing that there will not be room enough to store it. I will prevent pests from devouring your crops, and the vines in your fields will not drop their fruit before it is ripe," says the Lord Almighty. "Then all the nations will call you blessed, for yours will be a delightful land," says the Lord Almighty.**
—Malachi 3:10-12

WE LIVE IN ONE OF THE GREATEST NATIONS IN the entire world! Comparatively speaking, we really do live in a delightful land. We live in a land of freedom; we are not under oppression from our government; we are free to worship as we see fit, to work, to prosper; we are free to go about pretty much as we please. We have reasonable laws, and we have wonderful freedoms. I want to ensure we continue to live in a "delightful land"! The instruction for this type of outcome is in the Scriptures above. You are not only helping your own spiritual and financial well-being by being a consistent tither; you are also helping to ensure that our wonderful and blessed land remains that way. The more I read, study, and ponder these verses, the more I am passionate about the need for Christians to step up, raise their pens, write out their tithe check, and stand. Yes, we need to humble ourselves, turn from our wicked ways, and pray, and God will heal our land, but, we also have to be the ones to take up the gauntlet and keep running the race. We have to make the decision to give, and to keep on giving. Turning our faces like flint, we have to remain thoughtful of our ways and keep tithing to our local churches. We cannot look to politics or any other world system to keep our country thriving. Yes, those are important things—a strong military, a government of the people, for the people—but we as the church have to step up.

We can pray our Jabez prayer, do our 21 day "Daniel fast", we can humble ourselves and turn from our wicked ways, we can try to find our "purpose" in life, but there is a deep level of trust that is missing when we do not tithe consistently. What other way can we prove to ourselves that we mean what we say? That we really believe? Nothing else is measurable. I remember hearing on an old situation comedy the line "the last thing to be converted, is the wallet." We do ourselves a big favor if it is the second thing (second to our heart) to be converted! It helps to grow our faith!

Before I began my tithing journey, I *was* under a curse, and I could feel it! But I did not know why, though the televangelist knew that my generation had a small degree of education, knew a *little* about Malachi and about God promising to pour out His blessings on us. Now I look at it, and I understand it! Malachi was talking about consistent tithing, not a large and costly one-time, gift to some stranger living in another community, state, or possibly even another nation! Malachi talks about our local worship facility, and taking care of it.

Please write out your check <u>during the week</u> (or hold out your tithe as cash to the side) when you get paid, as well as when you receive unexpected income. Don't wait until Sunday morning and pull out the loose change in your pocket! Be ready and prepared!

Help keep your church not just afloat, but thriving. It takes resources; if your church does not get it from its members, where will it come from?

I challenge you to start tithing consistently now. Even if you cannot give a true tithe (a tenth), start with a ninth or a fifth or even, as Pastor Steve suggested, a "oneth." Just start! Work up to ten percent and be persistent, consistent, and tenacious!

Remember this skeptic's experience! Think on what I saw, what I learned, what changes were made in my life, and the blessings I am enjoying. Tithing is a law, but *you* have to set it in motion. No one can do it *for* you. Don't wait for your boat to come in; you won't ever start if you do that. Start tithing now.

Don't scream at the devil—just quietly raise your pen, write out that tithe check, and stand!